TREASON

BOOKS BY TERESE SVOBODA

FICTION

TRAILER GIRL AND OTHER STORIES
A DRINK CALLED PARADISE
CANNIBAL

POETRY

MERE MORTALS
LAUGHING AFRICA
ALL ABERRATION

TRANSLATION

CLEANED THE CROCODILE'S TEETH

TREASON

POEMS BY TERESE SVOBODA

ZooPress

Zoo Press • P.O. Box 22990 • Lincoln, Nebraska 68542
Printed in the United States of America

Distributed to the trade by The University of Nebraska Press
Lincoln, Nebraska 68588 • www.nebraskapress.unl.edu

Cover design by Dana Frankfort © 2002

Cover painting *Eyes* by Helen Lundeberg, 1942 © from the collec-
tion of Stephen Bull

Additional design work, LeAnn Jensen

            Library of Congress Cataloging-in-Publication Data

Svoboda, Terese.
  Treason / by Terese Svoboda.— 1st ed.
     p. cm.
  ISBN 0-9708177-6-2 (alk. paper)
  I. Title.
  PS3569.V6 T74 2002
  811'.54—dc21

                                              2002012452

zoo009

First Edition

Acknowledgments

Grateful acknowlededement is made to the publications in which these works orginally appeared:

88: "Nipple"; *AGNI*: "Sister Love"; *Alaska Quarterly Review*: "Khartoum Light" as "Khartoum Dinner Light"; *American Poetry Review*: "Agrarian Myth," "A Column of Whiteness" as "How to Save Yourself," "Cosmo Dog," "Fitting In," "Marriage Boat," and "The Unconscious"; *Atlantic:* "Belles Lettres" and "Aubade"; *Boulevard:* "Ghost House" as "Sudanese Ghost House"; *Columbia:* "At the Castle"; *Denver Quarterly*: "Flesh or Fetish," "The Cynic's Post," and "Highway to Heaven"; *Doubletake*: "Destiny Manifest"; *Field*: "Rule of K" and "Bridge, Mother"; *Grand Street*: "Extremist" as "Islam Extremist"; *Jubilat*: "Mr. Magneto"; *Kaimana*: "Harpies"; *Literary Imagination:* "Treason"; *Massachusetts Review*: "Crucifixion"; *New Republic*: "Sharon"; *"NORTH"* (U.K.): "Red Fox in Series" part I; *Paris Review*: "Report from High School," "Rock Polisher," "Sex and Class and Race," "Old God," "Anticipating Grief," and "Eurydice Abandoned in the Caves of Hades"; *Ploughshares*: "Money Can't Fix It"; *Prairie Schooner*: "Driving L.A." and "When the Next Big War Blows Down the Valley"; *Slate*: "Land's Cape"; *Poetry International*: "The Common Good"; *Tinhouse*: "Nickel Wife"; *Tinfish*: "On the Blown Marquee: Hurricane"; *Triquaterly*: "Pilgrim's Progress," "No Spring" and "Play"; *Turnrow*: "Two Dog Intersection"; *Verse*: "Statues of Women That Are Neither Angels nor Allegory"; *Volt*: "Peacocked"; *Yale Review:* "Death Stayed".

"Cosmo Dog" reprinted in the *New York Times Magazine* and *Unleashed*, ed. Hempel and Shepard, Crown Publishers, 1995.

"Bridges and Air" in *Stone and Steel*, ed. Bascove, David Godine, 1997.

"Death Stayed" in *Yale Review* and "Driving L.A." in *Prairie Schooner* reprinted in *Poetry Daily*.

To the constant

Table of Contents

III

IV

V

Suspicion all our lives shall be stuck full of eyes;
for treason is but trusted like the fox.
    —Shakespeare, *I Henry IV*

Play

It was customary in 15th century Italy
for the condemned to play the part of Christ.

You are not you, you are the Someone
on this mask and we are your followers,
we who applaud when you don't cry
or tear it off, when the noose
or the knife comes at last and our sins
rise with your soul that is better
than a beggar's, stealing butter.

Bridge, Mother

Mother burns on the other side of the bridge.
Mother burns the bridge and is safe on the other side.
Mother is not on the bridge when it burns.
When Mother says Burn, the bridge burns.
We can't get to the other side—
the bridge is burning.

Mother is the bridge that we burn.
She is how we get to the other side.
We can't burn the bridge without her.
Mother burns and we burn, bridge or no bridge.
She is the other side.
Nothing burns the bridge, and then it burns.

Statues of Women That Are Neither Angels nor Allegory

Relinquunt Omni Servare Rem Publicam
—after Lowell and Walcott

In Union Square her breasts are so full and stiff-
nippled surely she's nursing—or freezing.

Still she's Love. Three of my friends have no breasts.
What they have is five years until they get to die

like the rest of us. In the Icelandic saga,
women own as much as they can walk in a day. Every day

they walk. The Chinese say it's best to raise boys,
like the Greeks, like the couple, hands clasped,

deciding at the sonogram. Girl bones scatter the hillside
and yet—feel that man's touch, giving change,

hear the child's cry a foot away: *We want.*
What does Persephone say, the wheat queen's red-cheeked
        pioneer,

that compromised bitch strung out between husband and mother,
herself seasonless? The Chinese women unstrap

the toddlers from their backs to practice *tai chi*
in the park at dawn. At the other end, *Red Rover, Red Rover,*

little girls throw themselves over,
their arms shining with the medals of bruises.

In India, women videotape themselves working:
buckets of concrete balanced on their heads while holding

a child's hand, or weaving slats of plastic into chairs,
or stamping designs on silk over and over, then stop,

chapati for lunch, then stamp. The silk billows
fabulously around the shape of wind, the shape of life

lived after infant, after mosquitoes and fire ants
and nakedness and food. No one had ever seen them working.

Harpies

...the plague of Phineas
because he mistreated
his own children...
        —*The Aeneid*

The darkness of the city will be winged
and the wind rising from it will lift
the lost lists and newspapers as if

greeting the invading women
who will worry the smug family
where cruelty achieves perfect apogee,

lift by the nape those unworthy
of offspring, condemn them
to wastes where no expert can

absolve them. They will foul
the molester's food, use
the inverse of the mother impulse

to starve them.
O pagan angels,
the children are smiling,

collecting the lost drifting feathers,
hearing the rustling
in the closets of you

who will not be driven off,
whose shrieks ring the city in this
no–less–than–primal vengeance.

Eurydice Abandoned in the Caves of Hades

You hire a guide. See several waterfalls,
a dock for a boat, and—why not?—a boat.
You rock to a shore where bats rise as gulls.
Or fall. Such silence. You keep your head low,
wade black pools, one for each of the senses.
You light cigarettes, unnerved, defenseless
in the blue of that smoke. You see the roots
of trees, your sisters' hair unpinned, you see
it leads out. The sky! Then the guide rapes you,
steals your purse, and disappears. You really seethe.
Oh, god. Even Orpheus has lost it.
You can hear him through the rock, if that Shit!
is him shouting. You say, Let the stones drip
their milk. You'll sing louder, sing till you drop.

Cosmo Dog

The way all girl dogs talk French you'd think we
lapped wine and jumped hoops only in Paree.

But non. We are simply cats trapped in dogs,
trans-special, soon to travel to Den Haag

or somewhere with specialists (a species-ist)
who can free us from both this Gallist

lisp and this dreadful bark for which I think
they call us bitch. Twice I've consulted shrinks

on the subject of my name, to wit: Spot.
Run, Spot, run? they hmmmm. Think TV, think Spot

on prime time, you're the actress for Milkbone
who never ever thinks of drinking the cologne.

But it's "Out, damned Spot" over and over.
I sigh. At least it's a good author.

Sharon

I am the girl
whom you thought
would be male and muscled
from shoving off, encountering
cataracts, sudden shoals,
all the other watercraft.
Forget it. We float
and I kick those who moan,
those who lean so far
toward the fading shore
I have to pull ballast
and protect the lines.
We do a lot of fishing
on the crossing—after all,
dreams are just carp
under the surface
and you've got to eat—
and eventually
there's the singing to lead,
the handing out of oars,
and for some, the seasick pills,
all of which takes time,
what I'm here to spend,
that last trickle down the tub
that goes so fast.
A girl is good for this,
a man, trouble. He thinks what
he sees will save him.
It's still like that.
When the white light business
breaks, all I say is
we've been through a fog.
I thrust in my pole, I pull.

New Girl

Push me.
If I walk, it is to improve the carpet,
to let the nap from the TV
to the toilet rest. Ah, the *grossmutter*
folds her wings and you think
Travel Comportment, she behaves
herself. No. In California, only
the future behaves—it's fixed.
Crime, my dog, perhaps Pomeranian
or guinea pig, is fixed too.
He'll show you where we're going,
where lost gulls goof up,
flying legs down, like here's ocean.

The *grossmutter* likes the end of the board.
Yes, dear, where the shadow
and the water refuse each other, where
I like to bounce. See that palm?
The pool tickles it underground:
I've got seepage. Crime, fetch the rope
that pulls the plug, that's a good eunuch.
You'll see in a minute how the glugging
fits into my physics, what you came for.
Or was it Mehta-physics?
Mehta spent too much time
with her turban and wouldn't push me.

There's the baby. What do you get
when you cross a palm tree with a Pomeranian?
Return it. I once wrote a sentence the length
of that rope—it was like going underwater
to read it, the brain holding its breath.
A lot of German in the old *grossmutter*,

long sentences and what? A lot of appliances.
We Germans make a machine and make a machine.
Who can go back and find out why?
Smell my hands. Do old men smell like that?
Geese, maybe, fussing over spring grass,
pricked by chives.

Goose-Got! The old have only the young,
the young have themselves. You wouldn't guess
what my skirts hide. Let me lift them up
so at least I can drain my water.
Soon the guests will come to stare at themselves,
no swimmers either. They'll see what you see:
my gold afloat over blue, the Mother's colors.

Up in Flames

It's over now—
the little girl who wanted
a bicycle, the one needing
rent, the one without
whatever you have.

A model, to be able
not to ask. But even balls
held underwater
lose air

       bad air
trees change into good.

If I am not wood,
I could be tree—
when it is very very cold
they bleed.

Oh, put your arms
around me, Daphne.
The leaves are in lit mounds
all around.

How gorgeous the fall is!

The Morning Light and Its Rings

I am going through my mother's rings
in the morning light, each gem a planet

stopped on course, especially
the opal, a dinner ring of a size

she could hide behind. But she'll not be
found anymore, I think, tagging the ring,

If you dropped the stone in drink
they said it would dissolve

but it was Mother instead, who swam
so beautifully after, coif untouched.

Would I know how?
The shore is so far off

even the connection is bad:
I hear Failure, that whisper.

The opal goes opaque as if
daybreak blinds it, fire on fire.

I twist it on. Against my skin
it weeps blood and milk, all maternity.

Night Bird

In all the pictures she is sad.
It is as simple as this:
light comes through to pattern her
but she is dark.

When one of you calls,
she turns away,
the last gesture of hearing.

And at dusk, not night,
there is a sound torn
from the half-dark,
different from the others.
This is the way you go back.
Go back, she says.
And the picture is fixed.

Tsvetayeva

*Sent her two daughters to the
orphanage so they wouldn't starve.*

You were doing what was best.
For whom? Who had more food?
It took two weeks.

You would die without love.
Did someone steal their food?
The other wouldn't talk.

You couldn't hold a child
that light. You axed your wedding chairs
to bits so you wouldn't freeze,

then wept, grief good for what?
The bones and hair you came
to claim chained a noose

which worked wider and wider
until where you stood
didn't matter. Simple hunger.

Woman with God

           Just the ridged hat moving
in the six-foot-tall grass,
                     leaning windward,
    making the sun into coin, making
gold his search.
    And under it, his breathing,
and under that,
          the others.

Does god glance over his shoulder,
    feeling the breath of his followers?
    Blue Eyes, they chant,
    White Skin, and *Hat*, the ridged hat.

    Dios, the man swears, tripping in the grass.

She is picking beans when they ask
                 for virgins.
    She is so young her brother picks
    the top of the pole.
But she is not so young.
               She and her brother do play,
once in a pool—twice in a pool.
    Who knows? Go, they tell her.
      God waits.
           She goes.

          Gold or god? One letter.
But who spells it, and who reads?

The lost city,
as lost as heaven,
as his way,
as the river of metal hats peaked
as vulvas go on into the night,
and does not
stop for him.

A ghost march passes him
in the dark grass,
one man by one man,
each possessed, after centuries,
father after father,
possessed by gold,
and none of them hearing his fall from the horse.

She is made to eat
what he eats: the curled worm, toadstool
trapped in rotted dung, and dirt.
Manna or *manana* he calls it,
some sound.
God food.
The taste is not bad, she says.
She eats it all.

The horse lies sun–swollen and bird-thick.
He weeps before it, he bows,
touching the hoof,
then the shank
where the peavine wraps it,
tripping legs as long as a man's leg and arm together.

                    The tail,
bunched at the rump, shivers
        at his touch, a tendon unstrung.
            They see him, they see it,
            giant, a god's animal.

        How many days do they walk after
and around him, silent?
                Grasshopper Head, they whisper,
                near-blasphemy.
                            They put her with him,
the near-woman, and leave the grain
        to sour,
                    only so much of the moon left.
She says *Yes, this is Him*
                and she swings her hips
                as if already fruited.

                He is hunted—that's what he thinks.

The woman is bait.

                The rustling, the whispering
wells in the heat,
swells like his tongue stuck
to his cheek.
                He imagines himself meat,
        his own ear
                        the curl of a worm, him eating
him. But never god.
                        He takes what food they leave,
                        washes it in the river.

Gold lights the water
        until the river's silver.
                Clouds hang far off and arid,
and a worn moon,
                the whole world's moon,
                wipes the blue.

                        She stands
behind him, washing, washing,
                every move the same,
                she must learn all god's work.

Then he wades into the middle.
        He lies down with his hands out
                and it isn't like the horse wheeling
                at the snake and his falling,
the last shout of a compadre.

                                The death
uncurls.
                His hat floats.

                        And when she knows
what he's done, she shouts and points
to the grass
                so they turn away
                so she can say a cloud came

and strapped him to it,
                so she doesn't have to
        repeat his sinking herself,
                so she can stay
god-filled.
                        Though after the first grey,
                        the baby's eyes
                        go black,
                                her brother's.

Parents

The gods coo, so delighted you're helpless.
You beg to wear his boots, try on her dress.
All right. But first, work. And when you've built
a monument so high you think, *At last,*
let's negotiate—there's only static.
It's the stars, they say, it's your rhetoric.
Still, you have kindness, justice, love—fun.
They laugh behind their hands, two crows at noon.
What about the last and best wrapped gift—
immortality? There, my dear, you're really stiffed.

Treason

Perhaps, we whisper.
But who hears us? Who sees
what we do? Who tells?

The Greeks sally forth.
The vulture, the crow, even
the shrike spread their wings.

The gibbet's in place.
The beam and its triangle of support.
It takes three for treason.

We begat. It's always that simple.

Whisper that.
Three. Two to begat one.

The Greek goat
and a tree and the blood.
An army must eat. The secret
is eaten, it makes us grow.

All we have done:
sacrifice, then betrayal,
then justice. The cross or the gibbet?
Squint.

Then feast on the remains,
then cry. The Greeks with their poisons,
their good goat.

II

A Column of Whiteness

I am a small African woman
who opens her mouth and screams
into the dense burning foliage where
in a night made bright
I hide

from bucktoothed slaughter.
Weapons click in harmony
not far enough off. To say
I flee suggests I know my way.
I step over

sleeping students
who won't survive the fire
that, leaping in and out behind me,
they have set themselves.
Then I am mute

in front of an elevator which opens
to a column of whiteness in a suit,
and a woman less like my sex
than a bitch is. The big guns are now
in service

and I am not the only one
who hears, though I say nothing:
my jaws ache to eat death
like a rat its litter.
Swallowing,

I wish whiteness all over me,
and I am all white, the man offers
his tunnel out, the woman his hankie.
I am about to open my mouth Yes!
when what's approaching

makes them forget, leaves me
with myself, my white, white, white,
leaves me to the spit of the mob
that asks only
if I burn.

Crucifixion

Eighty-eight people, including two children...sentenced to death by hanging or crucifiction in Sudan.
 —*AllAfrica.com*, August 27, 2002

It's nonfiction,
a newpaper's open and shut.
But make that "suffocation,"
it's more genteel, the way

the limbs fail the lungs.
You want to read "a hill
full of crosses" but
Khartoum has no hills,

it's flat desert.
And it's not nails for the hands
and feet—it's staples.
Big staples. People prefer

the touch of technology.
Besides, you have to be angry
to pound, or have a lot of energy.
Who, in this heat? They're

all just criminals anyway,
or political prisoners,
Shell employees. There's
something about a post hole digger

working a cross into place
and the cross recycled,
the wood old-blood-sticky,
sandy, the flies.

Only occasionally do they
attach a footrest
to make it last longer.
Only occasionally

do they cut them down
and put them up the next day.
Only occasionally
are there no birds.

Pollution is catching up though.
Soon no scarlet-tailed hawk
or owl with tinfoil claws.
But who believes this?

Khartoum Light

It's pig you have to wonder about
I said, when venison showed. We drank
from the cafe's cup and spit
on the floor like the others.

I had no shoes so I crossed
the mound of dead deer instead of
the spray of glass that marked
the *souk*'s perimeters, shiny

as the flies coating the hides.
Then two men threw a bomb
and I bloodied my feet
running farther, but stopped

where the zoo emptied out.
Long ago all the animals had been eaten.
What I saw I looked at long,
as if caught by carlight.

Ghost House

Two million South Sudanese murdered in the last ten years.
  —Sudan Democratic Gazette

The ghost house holds up
walls but no roof so relief
drops the load right into
the kitchen, if the room
with bones is where one
would cook. The bones,
I've been told, pile up
in a ratio to the thickness
of birds that shoulder
each other in the shade,
big birds with names it seems
I made up then, long ago
when I was a guest
and it was roofed, the birds
not worth eating.
No one's eating now
anyway, the relief drop's
been exchanged for a woman
and when they're finished,
the house keeps her. I hear

they had my friend there
as a guest and now don't,
that they go out at night
looking for him, they crouch
with cigarettes
in the dirt fissures—
not even a ditch this time
of year—and the smoke
they make while they wait
is part of whatever Milky Way
that rises over us.

No Picnic

Beside us, oil rinses
the river. Or blood.

If I dig in the sand
will it drain to me?

That's foreign policy,
you say. We stare

at pipes ready to run
around the equator.

A hot shower
is all I need it for.

Well, they don't need that,
you laugh. From then on,

there's ants on the map
you must brush off.

At The Castle

To say one thing when your song means another.
    —Ezra Pound, "Near Perigord"

I phone Geneva, thinking Africa,
looking out the window at Italy.
The man who answers says they'll kill
each other, no one can stop them,
the UN demurs. Wine, that dark blood,
stings my nose. I take the phone

to the cliff where Pound said
nothing for ten years. You can't even
call the Sudanese, they can't agree
on a code. I say they're not starving,
the ones who are killing. You have to be
strong to rape and burn boys, boys

who sing in the dark all night,
troubadours wandering the savannah.
The wind arcs around the keep
and we both hear it. I hold
the receiver out over the battlements
and maybe the sound is someone

dying a European death,
German, Visigoth, Roman, Ice Man,
each stumbling over the bones
of the last, bones with meat
on them, bones Pound's great
grandson's dog fights for,

cur that he is. A paraglider hisses
over the pears, apples, grapes
cantilevering the slopes, taking
an exhausted loop over the spires.
Did you ever notice, I say,
how a city's most crowded cafes

offer cuisines from where the food's
most scarce? All the children under five
have starved in a province England's
size. Well, he says, the big boys
who are left, what they want is guns.
The wind falls in my silence.

Discovery

Here's rubber. He points to the tree.
Of course he doesn't say *rubber*—
the guy with the ax does. Or someone
at the Vatican, the backers. In fact,

explorers usually say drivel
in the face of wonder (Great view!
exclaimed spacemen). They smash
their mirrors to make better bargains,

the slivers eaten by natives who are just
homunculus unbottled to the guys-in-armchairs.
That they live there at all! As in war,
the beaters go first, to lure the lions,

then the women, so tea's ready
when he rests from his discoveries.
Who knows the way? He points, heavy pupae
borne by those who are home, or nearly.

Extremist

A train full of fire
and people
travel the horizon.

They say
Allah laughed
when he made
this country.

A train full of fire
travels the horizon
to its vanishing,
the very blue
I stand under.

Say it is as persistent
as a dream: I wake
and it's gone and it's not

Africa where flat earth theory
runs to hell—you can see
the curve, how the clouds
suck over, where the mind teeters.

A whole trainful burnt.
Hear His laugh?
Hear the soldiers'?

The land is bare now,
nothing to interrupt the sky,
nothing, not even dunes,
not even death.

Money Can't Fix It

My eyes must be open because light
through the woof of the hut's weave
shows my arm in pin shivers. What
wakes me?

A howl unfolds outside,
fear-in-the-mouth, a breathing trill
certifying the silence after. Sheep
in a barn as flimsy as mine

drum panic that my bones pick up,
an arthritis of fear. I stand, or at least
the dark and sleep leave on another level,
that kind of attention.

My story is half-heard and resented
in a bar where A-7 has played fierce
as a drill since midnight, where now
someone breaks something

and even the guy on my left
stops with his hands. When the cry comes,
there's this blip in the neon
we all watch.

Money can't fix it
says the jukebox, going on
while the glass gets swept.

When the Next Big War Blows Down the Valley

Flame casts the overhang in shadow
so no one can see anyone behind the clubs
or sharpened sticks each has made for himself
in the boredom of the many dusks when
the spilt blood has dried or sunk into
the red dirt at the bottom where food
grows and women dance and trees promise
drums and from where no one

ever escapes but takes up
the broken sharpened sticks and cuts
rows into the freshened earth until all they remember
of those from before is their small size,
and not their own good luck.

Report from High School

Where they sell greeting cards for jail
and use cops to keep us in
who've already been "in," where we write:

security is terrible but we can only spell
food, where just the super stays
for more than three months,

why not write about me?
asks the teenager with few teeth
and a smile to prove it.

There's a monster after me.
The bathroom's on fire, the tap's all gas
and rat guts and what I need

is a glass of water.
Yesterday the CIA recruited.
They want us and they'll give us

a roof to watch from.
Suck Sambo. The fire licking the dark
reflects us exactly. Write that.

Driving L.A.

Gas collects in the tunnels I drive through
until butterflies smoke on my car grill.

The gas is transparent but can find color—
see the spill in the gutter? It's an arrangement

of atoms, a matter of excitement. Take the video
of someone who's suddenly not transparent

but beaten and angry. I am not a person of color
and my soul is less, but I too am liable to

conflagration. As I pass roadside golfers
who whack at the flames that spew up the holes

fanned by police in low copters, I see
they can't see what's collecting.

III

The Listener Goes to Water

The silence water makes,
and waterfowl on their mark.

A made loneliness,
its stream runs uphill.

The dropped stone in water,
the cars in their circles.

Reflecting the bridge,
a skein of doubt.

And water tumbles down.
You had to open it.

A mad loneliness.
You had to, you had to.

Waves die, their reach is
not what it was, when it is.

You drive the wind
with the windows rolled.

Red Fox in Series

I

A squirrel like an interruption
of weather wets our hunter in socks,

his black lips. Red fox advances through
primrose which shouldn't be, should be
field or orchard with mice, shrew
and pigeon. Red fox at least goes

on all fours, red fox looks to be
growing out of the ground a shoot
at a time, a change of season
all at once,

taunt, a circuit red from eartip down,
every animal moment spent in live histories
of fox Rome, fox Greece
with the arc of light the tail makes—
not the imagined tail—
spent and worth it.

II

A woman
in a courtyard
not yet rented,
with vines coiling over love,
a left thing,

the woman spreads
her things. The courtyard
holds shadows where
a man comes
and has been. Rome leaves—

dappled, bright green—
     but Rome cannot, the whole courtyard
     grown from it,
its day fallen.

     Goats charm the woman
or seem to, she sees them on the stair
and not
     you, seeing. Shut the house
and rent it,

     as wild as Rome, as root and vine.

III

They fumble for a keepsake for the sake
of a minute, of a Do you know it's name?

of a gunnysack tight with rock bits,
of a voice calling Delivery.

All well and good, the biblical,
the out of touch—where's the fur?

Kids are crying Fax, fax when they mean
fox, when they mean they don't know

when their hand is in the bag.
Could it be the belly, its entrails

coiling, and not wiring,
the fur of old food

they're inside of? They know
nothing yet, they take delivery.

Flesh or Fetish

A critic is thinking up praise.
One Narcissus, two Narcissus.

All that the mind holds atrocious,
glory fingers—and adores Echo,

the faltering anorexic, but does
she sing of flesh or fetish?

And what of the cloud that covers
the deadly boring? A fine varnishing,

a fat varniska. With admiration
for the teeth, N. yawns

in duplicate. Remember the cloak
in the story, the cloak, the cloak?

The love bolt? The perfect
vision? Gut vs. head?

Still drowned, the phone
off the hook or hard rung.

The Cynic's Post

is tall and notched
with disappointment.

You say: with appointment.
The cynic promotes taste

in plaid, one hot
against another,

and a fence for the rest.
Into the Pacific sinks

a square green sun and our post
measures this green. It is still

a sunset, though cynic green
isn't natural, surely the weather—

your eyes and not the sun pours
in the appearance, it is all

appearance: a pear is the earth's
central figure, true shape

and shadow. You squint, you see
green swallow your hands.

The post squares the green
as it goes down, yes, as it sinks

the unsuitable goes, with the dark
next, making the cynic now the past,

dug in sand with doubt-shifting.
You turn your back to all of it.

A post is a dog's, for pissing.

The Answers

The President nauseates.

The cell gets banned, "gets"
verbs its way into the body,
begets.
                      The President
cuts his tongue.

             Propagation.
But phoney, that tongue,
a million of them, wireless
unless the President throws up

his hands at blood.

What an explosion!
Each cell has its say:
each to his own, each,
then, disposes.

              The President
makes us sick. See cells
by the seaside? You
call in the answers.

Drink Beer until You're Handsome

Your life's on a stick and held up
like a god's. No taxes for you,
and what Death answers
you pickle in an egg. Growing wiser,

the stick salted but still good,
you meddle, you pay them to keep going.
Them is the Great Mother's dreams
of you as a child, the spyglass

reversed, the land they discover
while you keep going. That
you could learn is what
they've forgotten. Drink,

drink, don't cry at the rail
where the body of you-know-who
is wafered out. You will be handsome
on that stick, then you are.

The High Cost of Principle

Shadowed by a dog,
     the infinite dog, mirror of all
in all the leaves,
        I bark faithfully
because we are one
        and the cherry pie offering
that glistens in the snow,
     organs he's left after the kill,
the jays disagree on.
               Still I walk
        into where the birds aren't,

with the principle wagging the dog
     in my forebrain. If there were
no dog, says the dog, circling,
     making a kind of floe
        with his prints cutting through,
the fruits would be gathered this day
     same as the next. Thus
        the dog offers his neck.

The Comfort of TV

We find the sails we are not
looking for in the tablecloths
too late to spread for our meals of hunger,
the food unplanted beside the furious worm's
weavings who alone ties the dirt down
against wind that could not be,
even on TV.

The Unconscious

Madagascar's Aepyornis Maximus, *extinct in the
16th century, was once the largest bird in the world.*

Where, in the dunes,
is the roc shell, in shards
the size of my mirror?

According to Marco Polo,
these birds lifted elephants.
Why, I wonder, pocketing

bits. Souvenirs?
On this island, spiny things
surround all the prizes,

pirate scapula, cats, cactus.
I hack at huge succulents
whose thorns lace the path

of the last known longitude
and my guide's best guess
to heat-sense the sand

for eggs, the optimistic eggs
that so many chickens,
so many ostriches,

fit inside. Of course, they're empty.
Imagine the ham-sized haunches
running—not flying—

into fires set by whom,
to turn on what spit,
the last grease

licked from whose fingers,
licked and licked.

Peacocked

        In the dusk light screams—
no, calls

       Between the prongs
of the turnstile—spread feathers—the boy's head

Raise your arm
   Under it, that arc
           fly
    hens like turkeys
to the boughs—
           ballast—
    then legs

Bent and reversed
    feathers break the display

Color-stumped
    oil drained from water

Fire one. Fire two. A salvo

        What did you say?
     The letter's lips ripped
those ruffles
   a strutter's

If white isn't available
   chose multi, chose all

        The turnstile turns

    The spit dances on its stick leg
             screams

   Please

The Horse in the Garden

The ball leaves your hands. Ha,
ha, ha. Levity leaves too, the sky
is full of it. Why are we waiting
at the gate when we could be—

we could be— The horse makes
an effort and the rider sits
in thrall. The airborne sky
against the gate, the gate hit.

Ha. The ball against us,
the game rules while we wait.
The rider, a great Polish fellow,
laughs, undeterred, teetering.

Don't let him in. Wait. The horse
hoofs the sky. You don't play.
You wait with us. Ha—you
wait? The game gives out,

a bit here, there. A garden
grows up, lost balls roll
for the sure-footed, for those
who wait. The horse takes the gate.

The Plants Revolve

Not planets stuck on
with gum, not space
and its evident lack,
its crowd of trash,
its lit fires, cold
cold. You think

you're a plant and me
the sun, as mixed up
as that, sputtering
under a watering
can of tears just because
you can't get away.

Dirt is some big magnet,
home is where the heart
stays buried. You twist
on your stick, a rack
you've made here and
nowhere else, you twist

to the sun of enterprise
(tick, tick, the organism
contracts, not enough
celery turgor).
Enterprise surrounds you
like the sound system

in a movie where you hear
the polite cough
of industry in your popcorn,
the faux sun at your back
projecting at you alone.
Inside, the real inside

where space is mindless
and attention drifts
into great shoals of triste,
we turn separately, fearlessly,
non-concentrically, the blades,
the blades almost upon us.

Curse the Fish into Wishing

The river's in slats, the slats animate it
as if moving in a movie, the slats are:

grocery store, prison gate, doctor car, eye lint.
Where your eye catches you looking over the river,

the river shines all too visible to the fish, air-borne.
You snag chinbone hooks as he flips, he wears hooks

you could lean on with big clippers. Big fish.
The movie runs awhile, the river runs.

Food shrugs its tiny shoulders up to the fish face.
The fish nods more into the hook but Hey

you could eat worm, you could eat that marabou tuft.
The river still runs and the fish with you

stuck to it, your arcing line glistening a U
over the slats, the Everglades blooming,

the movie not in the least released.

Signal

So far as I can see, my effort continues.

Two men ride west and their buttocks,
their mounts smooth it out.

The Go West sign suggests more than just
a left turn for them, it suggests

my effort. They ride when I tell them.
I am embarrassed to tell them but

it is for them that I do, I am a saint
to tell them. It isn't so bad,

I tell them, but they don't believe me,
they take their mounts further in than

anyone, or further out, depending on
where I am left holding the bay

of honesty. As they venture,
as their horses climb into that blue,

as they reach cloud and climb on,
I watch their buttocks.

IV

Mr. Magneto

Mr. Magneto leads a love life: attract, repel. The fun wears out and then the wind blows and Mr. Magneto removes a clot of wax from his ear.

Of a size. Others of his ilk, inventors of glue guns and cat catchers who suffer love drive or have, with the clutch of a life slipping and their own ears rattling with wax make their impressions.

Mr. Magneto presses the wax against his member and the wind blows.

Standing beside, or enough beside his car he cannot open it without member damage, he sees his electromagnetic field, a vision of poles in perfect line-up, legs kicking, matches crossing metal covers.

It is not so much the whole car he stands beside but important parts one thinks one would want but would soon learn to do without, in the heat of magnets, and flame.

The others who don't learn but lend themselves to learning, also stand beside the car.

The boy sliding the magnet thinks well of them, he even has one of them jump, jump at the flame like a dog.

The car comes out of the flames and he pounds it with a stick sharp with stone until it takes on a shape.

Mr. Magneto gets into the newly shaped car the way you do after it's just been detailed and herds the rogue or dumb others together.

Sirens blare, wax melts.

You don't listen, says the older person to the boy and the boy looks up, the magnet on its string swinging.

On the Blown Marquee: Hurricane

We whimper for chips
to quell our anxiousness. There,
             the water's lining up:
wave, wave, skip.
             We want to surf in the math,
then the aftermath as they say
on the tube,
             or after school
which is closed and sluiced,
             the kids on the beach.

    Mostly there's congratulations
             for the silver twitching planes
and their touchdowns and—let me see—
             no domestic violence.
Not on the planes, of course—no in-flight
    movies now—but under the barometer,
    the mistletoe of home as fort,
where the windsock's shot.

    So put up the blankets,
put up the beer,
             the surf's soon surfeit
though we ourselves
    little enervate the weather
             with our lust.

Who Goes with Whom?

Every night, lick lip.
Every day, suppress chest.
I'm up to here
with chest, with flirt—
not too far.

They've designed a flower
that's transparent. You can see
the parts crossing with the Mayday!
Mayday! of spring.

Napkins cover my lap,
more than one, and white ones.
The pleasure is surely just Hi!
you've got me, you don't have to
touch that.

I'm up to here
with something that's braided.
If it unravels,
color won't be lost,
just pattern.
(Fire's bright in the blood.)

It's a game:
many denominations
and colors,
counterfeits that play
like the others. The purpose
is who goes with whom and then

it's not over.

Marriage Boat

Gulls ogle and swoop those in the boat,
even those with children, even those

with eyes fixed as figureheads.
Flesh! Flesh! the birds scream.

Rope is not the operative word here
but line, as sex alone suggests

sibilant potential, not love.
At any time the stern could disappear

back to where it came from,
the clouds herding their foam away

from reflection. Yet it seems, on clear days
when no one's crying, it seems

as if the boat bears both ocean and sky,
and the bodies fly, hiked so far out.

The Silence of the Tortoise

He has his back to her.
She scrabbles up.
There it is—the field,
the double lanes.

Cutting the ears off
hares—is this
a sign? Left, right
or yield? The hares

don't listen anyway,
he says. They never care
how a race is won. She says
the he tortoise grows long arms

to clasp the shes.
You're not so old, he says.
But the silence after, the shell
falling against the glass.

Aubade

Sinews here and there,
his legs twined at desk
and all of him bare,

mousing around, click,
so the child won't wake.
Sinews, his sex thick

but laptopped, glasses
found then lost then
a child flushes

and my hands on him
count only as clothes,
as information.

Sinews, I say, *sotto voce*,
and he smiles into
his screen. At me?

Nipple

A smaller dollop of people
and we could pass.
But even with arms akimbo, no.
Instead, we throw our heads clear

and there's the moon.
You reach up and cup it.
People push past us—they do, they do—
and we could be leaves

filled and lifted
among them
except the light is
what lifts us,

moon enough for everyone.
But only you
brushed it,
so hard and full.

The Nickel Wife

You don't hear their words
turn dull, his third glass
empty. You don't hear

Hate either, only talk
in a cove, lust talk,
the way you remember it.

A life of two circles,
is circling when you show,
the nickel wife. More drink

is thus necessary
to throw the coin and still
see it, unspent, at the bottom

of all this. But the water grows
darker, the talk too, it grows
out of anything anyone says,

a cloud but no stars. You drive
her home—no—she does the long
alcohol exhale and time

evaporates, the island
rocks as never before, the seals
swim across and back,

the little bird
just not coming
to the top.

Belles Lettres

Slowly, slowly, so as not to awaken
himself, he scratches his ear.

The sun is out, that is, not.
Sheets and her rucked-up slip

line his back in canals (a misunderstood
Martian) where sprout and curl hairs

as rogue as he is, shrugging off
the phone call assault,

the covers coming over in waves.
Does he growl, Nice night

in bed, or, sniffing, It could rain?
He's reading her instead.

The Common Good

Imagine democracy believed in,
as common as a cold, not washing
your hands so it will spread,

the man in your bed so democratic
he's another people, watching you
insert your contacts and a horror

surfaces and he enters you
to hide it, with a lack of
tenderness you could not expect.

You see now the effect of democracy,
this man you love abstract suddenly
in his so fascinating fear of

your eye going in, and a desire
that makes you common shakes
the two of you, unbelievable.

Endymion

A thing of beauty is a joy forever—
—Keats, "Endymion"

The moon keeps the man young
by keeping him sleeping.

Coma is a moon word: she
is the moon of his eyes,

that close. Keats pursued
the Indian maiden

who must not be caught
for she is "Immortal Love

like Brain-Flies leaving us
fancy-sick." The young man

runs between the trees
with unexposed paper,

hot for moon-stroke. Soon
she is fixed in the bath forever.

Yet night after night,
his children tumble as he tumbled,

in search of some blonde.
A thing of beauty is just as

described. But not the Indian Maiden.
They see their father ahead

with his art, deaf to the cry
in the dark that it's over.

Fitting In

In Saudi Arabia
the plane is not late, the taxi
is and all these children I have
will not fit in.
      Say they are blossoms and reasonable-sized
      and lizards from such deserts as this
      fork them—petals all over the place.

Our luggage gets chalked in swirls.
I think cloud patterns, what we're in for,
or sand. A sandbox with sides this
isn't. The plane leaves a syrup
of fuel where it can't take off,

then it does. Once on the walkway,
      the children stalk the lizards.
      The lizards have petal-shaped scales
and one eats his, loosening the fit
around the mouth, tonguing the scaly
transparency inside.

      The children see this as good,
a silicon chip breakfast, smart food smarter
than pumpkin pie for hackers, their heroes.

              They bloom while I
give out shovels
from the trunk of the taxi
and—what do you think?
      They hit each other over the head,
quarrelling.
            Then they fit.

At What Cost

Bosomed-boy-my-own, old
as the hormone flush which is
eight, no more, the TV beloved
is too high to be doused its light,
given the height of the terminal
we can't leave these seven hours,
all unslept and fretting. At no cost

will I let you go, will I will it
yet the plane will be fixed,
my tears dried, your bosoms
flattened. Run me over
with your toothy front tire,
oh Chapter 11 Boeing, we can't
afford this or a new ticket.

But we can and do, in darkness,
the cry queen bolted ceilingward
summons a preacher's voice
from a deeply pleasureable place
like the stewardess'
when she closes the gate
before my lingering, my long stare.

Pornography Is Good

His side has its points,
all researched. Winning, he says,
means money, beer if whoever's brother will buy it.

If the sides come up equal, what tips
the balance? Right is might, he says.
You're hiding the car keys.

Where do you stand on this, with the absolutes
firing their unison guns? Pleasure
is a principle, like math. Welcome to the wiring

of say vs. do, where the glass elephant trumpets
and salvos hit the unseen side of the moon.
He walks a nice line, drunk on all those knows.

Rock Polisher

A worm
inside this one, he says.

Over and over he grinds it,
an unclear oval of brown,

its edges rough and grit.
The polisher echoes.

Hollow perhaps, he says.
Except for the worm.

Among the rubies

it lies, among smooth gravel.
We think dragon
but he means

anger. What else do boys
conquer?

Held to the light so,
and away,
the tail flicks.

Gone Wave

The wet sand, scoured, shows
plant-green hair I could swim through
but not save.

I could dream this
as prophecy. I could forget.

        I suction
my sand-heavy suit
off the surf floor.

The next wave,
lens-clear, holds
the boy up in more
light than wave,

each eyelash
separate, the arm-bend
not right.

I spit foam, press water
with my hands.

He rises again,
just about to be born, to be borne—
Mother—

now and no more.
The last wave a looking away
in so much water.

No Spring

Let me die when I do
in dead winter so
you'll be sorry while
it's dark and cold while
I'm ditto.

He died on the year's first day
of no coats, of running
to the window to look
out below. Nothing
much saved him and

no thick fur or sweater
will save me these shivers,
just season on season.
So what if spring's
new. A bird

falls on the walk I make
to warm up. I squat to it.
Chick, chick, chick, it says
from its broken neck,
no spring left.

Sex and Class and Race

Books say parents
didn't mourn their children

in previous centuries, that
nose-wipes and infants

died as eidelweiss on a granite face,
so much sex in excess.

But at the very least, the poor
had their need for labor.

Perhaps the rich left children
to wolves or footmen,

perhaps they saw a child
as a purse divided.

Perhaps.

But even their women ran
into the snow, not to return,

or cut something again and again
so it wouldn't mend.

Yet people do forget.
Even I forget,

blind in the dark passage,
bent as the Victorian foliage

that screens me from them,
so sepia-dirty in their sullen

photos they might be another race
if color is what it takes

to dodge such sorrow.

Release the Gifts

—for J. and A.

The fumbled Yes, as all your life
passes before you, quick-time, the expedient

shore looming, means Why not? Your complicated faces
we could put on a card. Congratulations

it would say and Bear witness! You execute
several excellent wedding steps

and far exceed any relative's shuffle,
we who stay put, blocking the sister

gripping her thinness. If one should prosper,
must another shrink? Friends screen the answer,

rallying with the remnants of your bouquet,
and drink so you can take flight as one.

We're just fuel, fossils all, you youngest.
There's plenty of gravity to go around.

Longing to Stop Longing

—for Elizabeth

You fill it
with different colors of sand.

When it runs out, there's grey,
a feigned blindness.

The dog chases the rabbit
and the rabbit leaps.

It doesn't turn to check its dog.
Memory chases.

"Still mourning" reads the sign
in the yard after the hams stop

coming. It's God dressed in a peasant blouse
atop steep clouds who rains down

another storm of sand. Are you sure?
Shshshshsh, the rabbit's stopped,

ears up, and a white
shapes its waves around it.

Bridges and Air

Once we wove two trees'
boughs into bedsprings
to meet over a river.
Once in a desert

caravan, two weeks passed
while Who Goes First?
got talked out and tried.
Once we pulled up our feet

and held our breath.
The fret can't fail, can.
Every bridge has its child
ghosts in the supports,

their pipes wavering
as the bricks set,
new shoes and hat added for luck,
whatever they never lived to get.

The strongest bond,
the biggest sacrifice.
In a moment of bridge,
that blue yawns wide.

Pilgrim's Progress

You run toward a light.
A cartoon idea?
Running forces its burning,
fuels its whiteness.

Such light capitalizes:
All Good as in a cafe.
Each lifted sole
is a moon left on.

No one said you had to run
or that the race raised money
but if, by running,
you actually arrived—

the dead light of stars
wink and go out.
Still, your organs swell
as you run, you want

and want but you can't stop.
Your side aches,
your head aches,
your heart.

Friends wave slick magazines
that read Relax,
friends with a capital F,
in the plural, but not the humble,

declarative friend
whose hand you slap
as you pass—he's hunched,
he's just laced up.

Sister Love

I'm underground and there's a drip.
It could be calcium, it could be sorrow.
The dark, though, suggests self-pity.
Who's breathing?

                    My brother on his blue satin.

It's as if all my life I waited
and the wait did it. Here, it's underground
                    and cold and

I'm driving and mist breaks around me
so I have "something to show,"
meaning my body. It's not
that I put on those rubber gloves
backwards, Orphee in Cocteau,
or even get out of the car—
                    fire explodes in the slick
                    as I pass.

Surely he puts on his gloves
and goes to work, clumsy as ever.

The way sugar sets hunger is enough
to imagine what sets death. Imagine
the cave alive, lava surging,
an excited sorrow
                    because I said so.

Death Stayed

It feels like creation,
walking in on dogs
in their caged life and

pointing, that spark
ordained, "God
and man joined as animals,"

when we pick. Clouds
roll up and down the lot,
enchantment really,

as the dog jumps at my wrist
to kiss or tear. You open up
and tell me what it feels,

the third that makes the drama,
the queer addition
animals offer, our motion

of picking life off a seesaw
up now above the clouds,
the car climbing home,

our corporal selves
writ again,
with death stayed in a dog.

Duet

        The dolphins
only twice in real life
     bumped boats in warning.

    The emptiness of the water
         means they're hiding, not
that the dolphins can't see us.

If they look like sharks,
imagine what we resemble.

Lay your ear to the water.
     Are those pleas for a human Lassie?
The sound cuts through our splashing.

    With no one to define what life is,
let alone real, you sing along,
       a *karaoke*, you sing
         for someone to save you.

Land's Cape

Think water, its diamonds
on the brink of sinking,
a pleasure boat, Pleasure
painted—*ital.*—midhull,
a cold glass thrust up
to shore—highrise at sunset—

its bubbling fast,
        the short life of ice,

the sand, with its hilly secrets,
a rug of weed thrown over
backyard trash, and a spigot
of leaves screening what
the sun might do
to a lettuce plume.

Root Canal As a Venetian Idyll

The exhausted dream I live in
    is scattered with teeth, the little
        tombstones of Freud that,
plowed under,
        grow up warriors.

        My son buries his
between pillow and case so no one
    can exchange them for
foundling dollars—
        he wants to string them together,
        the miser.

The rule is you lose a tooth for every child.
    The new baby grinds,
        gnashes, butts
at the inexplicable ache inside—
        the dog that won't shake off.

    Yet he gums prettily between howls.
So smile! repeats his jack o'lanterned brother,
        as I do, falsely,
            as Death does.

Anticipating Grief

It is both the coffin-worn hammer
and the hassle we walk under,
sans spouses, those shields
and mirrors of the family fantasy.

It is both, and we cry as if truth
changes when wet. When we speak
into the long tunnel ahead, we are heard
but the hearing takes time, maybe

we will die first. Oh, who can
die first? It's another family game,
each with his own blank screen.
When some echo of triumph

leaks back to where the spouses
wait, it's mixed with
an Esperanto of guilt
they invent, feet tapping.

How to Simplify Fractions

Put the big one
over the small one
and what do you get?
Don't tell.
He was a big man
and the first time
the boy cried.

Sometimes the wounded
use their scars.
Pull up the small one's
sleeves now, see all
the lines,
fine white
at the wrist,
where the answer goes.

The Rule of K

Give someone a name beginning with K if you want a hero.
—Neil Simon

In the dead body:
　　　　my brother, doppelganger.
Look over
my shoulder:
　　　　　　he too was paranoid.
　　　　　　　　But what's
natural cause at forty?

　　　　At night he'd open
the first volume and read:
Aardvark, earth pig, 3 $^1/_2$ feet long,
　　　　then read to K,
　　　　　　then sleep.

　　　　K's the vitamin
they give you if you bleed.
　　　　I had K in Africa,
miscarrying like a pig,
　　　　some other lady
dead without it,
　　　　　　the double.

　　　　What divides me from him—
eleven months
eighteen days—
will never close.

　　　　But who was that fat Karen
after his money and why
did he keep a crippled cat
　　　　　　he couldn't catch?

The sound of K multiplies.
Christ, another paranoid,
        with a name you can hear
from every pew, was born again
in the month he died.

                I need a hero.
Hear the cat
        he couldn't catch,
crying for liverwurst?
What's worse than liverwurst?

        My brother ate it
to prove he wasn't me.
Now, surely, he's not.

Mother Bleeds from the Mouth

The ocean laves one long line
where the sun sets how red?

My hand waves at it,
all meaning wry

since no one's around.
Around and around a scarf

beats in the sunset wind,
DNA against cloud.

Maybe my hand waves for that.
Maybe I should speak.

The ocean closes and closes.

Old God

Ah, to be old and rage uncontrollably,
to command the sun and moon to stop
and yet be treated like a dog,
house training at ten and two
or we'll weight your walker. Flatline

the sun does daily, and the dog
howls anyway. I read where men's bodies
can be made twenty years younger,
only men's—we're so simple. I totter
toward a diamond of yellow light,

where the same geese snatch bread
ad nauseum. No one wants to see
them past their prime—they fly elsewhere
for their duplicate unsexed deaths.
Why feed them? I parade,

leg by leg, back to my barracks,
my rage rising over a horizon
of sleeping nieces. Weep wombs,
for what you hold is
not yourself, over and over.

Agrarian Myth

—*for J.S.*

Father says Come. A hundred years
of fathers, hundreds. You stand
on the flat of yourself, not the cornfield
or the half acre in rotation.
You can hear him, you've taken

psychology, you have watched
him tip up the 4-wheel drive.
Aren't my feet yours? he says.
He says, Look at the land underneath.
But you succor a whirlwind

that lifts and lifts.
Whatever's on your hands won't
wash off into the dirt.
It could come from dirt.
A spider crosses your father's

letter, the acrobat's answer.
When you cartwheel into the air—
no land at last—Father will take
his cap off in time to the music
and money will fill it.

Great Circle Earthworks, Ohio

*Remnant of prehistoric Ohio, nearly 1200 feet in diameter,
used as a vast ceremonial center.*

I could be a teen,
thinking Mystery, that delicious
void, or I could be older,
puzzling out life in a light rain
and why it won't wash.

This Circle is no Cheops
nipple, just displaced dirt,
a sculpture too cheap to steal,
protected by huge trees
lightning-drawn like Woodlawn's.

Another race built walls
two stories higher in Hawaii.
Or do the walls just seem taller,
height so relative to my own age and wear?
I look out from the center toward

Hopewell, the nearest settlement,
where the mutt American's plough erases
every planting, god so much on his side
he doesn't need history. Knock, knock?
is what his mounds repeat.

A white horse gallops
the Circle's rim, only a few tricks left.
The shape of the future's an hourglass—
the shape of god? We moon him
with a mound.

Destiny Manifest

Your fence meets your fence,
the sawtooth borders contiguous.
You can't even see it all.

Shade moves its bars like latitudes
across the no-tree, no-cow plain.
Land is plain, unwrit and lasting.

You long to envelop the map
with circumference.
I have seen you look down and

look up like that, in such lust.
Your binoculars pick out antelope
that move no closer than x power,

that canter back as if there's a line.
Like the concentrics of the eagle
a thermal over. Like water after a stone.

Healing Wind

—that's upwind, where
genealogy has swept its O's
and X's beyond

hugs and kisses.

This week is not
the last, your sister implores.
We stand at the tap, pails

filled, the wind in ruffs
so no reflection
shows. She's not especially

cold but the chill index says it all:
worse than you think.

No one cries.

Why
tempt sisterliness
when there's loss to carry back, lots
of it?
We heft and tuck our heads.

Bacchae

The horns of the barbarians
review their scales.
> Again.

She could gather and crush berries,
brew
> to soothe her exile, but no.

> Her small cry
disturbs no butterfly,
> no wind rises, no echo pretends
an answer from elsewhere.
Sorry.
> She drank and debauched,

> she tore her own son
into quarters with just her hands,

her feet on his neck. Women do this.
A drink at four, loud ice
> then trick him
up a tree, shake the trunk.

> When she hears him fall,
she runs to catch him—
but you cannot both birth and catch.

She bears up, a queen even.
She bears him. She unbears him.
The head, with its roots raining.

Sanity blinks.
> The barbarians play.

Elsewhere
              in the day room
          women weave a song
              of small cries
into patterns,
into a kind of plaid

that a schoolgirl would wear
wrapped too short,

              the kind of girl who prays

that no one
will see the spot in that plaid
              when she rises,
that the blood will somehow
get back inside her,
              a wound
she understands she must

smile through
              until that's all anyone sees,

              the miracle of motherhood.